MARRIAGE:

Until Death Do Us Part

MARRIAGE:

Until Death Do Us Part

J. MARTIN

WESTBOW·
PRESS
A DIVISION OF THOMAS NELSON
& ZONDERVAN

WestBow Press books may be ordered through booksellers or by contacting:

WestBow Press
A Division of Thomas Nelson & Zondervan
1663 Liberty Drive
Bloomington, IN 47403
www.westbowpress.com
1 (866) 928-1240

Because of the dynamic nature of the Internet, any web addresses or links contained in this book may have changed since publication and may no longer be valid. The views expressed in this work are solely those of the author and do not necessarily reflect the views of the publisher, and the publisher hereby disclaims any responsibility for them.

Version of the Bible used is: New King James Version-The New Open Bible Edition Thomas Nelson, Inc. 1982/1990

Any people depicted in stock imagery provided by Thinkstock are models, and such images are being used for illustrative purposes only. Certain stock imagery © Thinkstock.

ISBN: 978-1-4908-2385-0 (sc)
ISBN: 978-1-4908-2387-4 (hc)
ISBN: 978-1-4908-2386-7 (e)

Printed in the United States of America.

Library of Congress Control Number: 2014901446

WestBow Press rev. date: 02/07/14

Contents

Dedication

To my wife Gloria, a jewel and saint, who has encouraged and assisted me every step of the way while writing this book.

Acknowledgements

May I extend my warmest gratitude to Elder William & LaJuan Elston, Jr. who has wholeheartedly supported our marriage ministry for the past fifteen years? Furthermore, I want to thank Mrs. LaJuan Elston for voluntarily doing most of the typing and proof-reading the material in the manuscript, for which I'm very grateful.

I am genuinely indebted to Bishop James M. Scott, Sr. for allowing us to teach the material in this book annually (since 1996) to couples at the Holy Temple Cathedral Church of God In Christ. A special thanks as well to Mr. Lebron Cathern for assisting with the artwork on diagram 2, *Climb Your Mountain to its Peak*. Credit goes to Mrs. Rhonda Seeber for designing the paper cover for the material we used in the marriage workshops. She was so eager to help make the workshops successful with such a colorful paper cover. Without any doubt, a heartfelt appreciation goes out to the West Bow Press staff especially my check-in coordinators, Austin Eblen, Paul Hatley, and Shaun Kauffman; and to everyone else who contributed one way or another in bringing this book to fruition. Last of all, my deepest and sincerest recognition unequivocally goes to my late mother who always believed in me.

Introduction

As we enter the 21ˢᵗ century, the institution of marriage is crumbling before our eyes. For in various courtrooms across America and other countries as well, the foundation of the covenant marriage according to the biblical view is disregarded and substituted with **"trial marriages" "common law marriages" "open marriages" "serial marriages"** and **"same sex marriages."** Marriage is seen as a way to fulfill one's sexual desires, as well as an expedient way of accumulating material goods. It is no longer a command from God, but a human choice if deemed necessary. It has become a haven for abuse, adultery, rebellion, enslavement, and entrapment. Even the male/female position in marriage has become interchangeable; and misleading thousands of newlyweds each year. In many places in the United States, our legislators and politicians have campaigned to eradicate this sacred and holy institution by sending it before the Supreme Court. As this piece of legislation went before the Supreme Court, the act of marriage is redefined, to include the same genders as being equal to husband and wife. This shows how far we have departed from God's original plan for Adam and Eve, or Mr. & Mrs. Adam. In God's plan, marriage is between a man and woman, and should be built on companionship, not selfishness; peace, not confusion; commitment, not resentment; until death do us part, not when we depart. But now, the institution of marriage is just a sideshow with farcical characters displaying ungodly principles and ignoring the guidelines God formerly laid for the bonds of marriage.

The aim of this book is to show how God has positioned the man and woman in the institution of marriage so it will last a lifetime. Too many times couples confuse their position with their role. The word position is an act of placing or arranging in order, but the term role is the part a person plays in life or literally from a roll of paper on which an actor's part is written. If God isn't the author of the script, then your marriage is out-of-alignment and will fail unless it's realigned. What God have arranged for marriage is permanent and those who interfere with His arrangement are held responsible to the utmost. So if the body of Christ expects to resolve this marriage crisis, they must first begin inside the church and then emanate it to every neighborhood, city, and state to change the nation.

Breaking Point: A Marriage in Crisis

Isaia and De'Borah Sarrmon lived their lives as an ideal couple, and is now preparing to celebrate their fifteenth anniversary only 18-months away. They're successful black entrepreneurs who work diligently to provide a good home for themselves and their two children. It's a home that has all the amenities and comfort of a suburban town house. They both enjoy working in their local church as youth leaders of a large group of adolescents. De'Borah, a 40 year old Educator at Rich-Mann University, is always volunteering her services to the church, whether giving of her time or finances. Meanwhile, Isaia, a 36 year old Christian Counselor/CPA, discovered another business venture he thought will make a great investment. After giving it some consideration, Isaia decided to invest $150,000.00, most of their life saving from a mutual fund investment that yielded them nearly $200,000.00 over a 10-year period.

In addition to his new investment, Isaia found the perfect vacation cottage he wanted to purchase as a surprise anniversary present for his wife (De'Borah). But in order to do so, he had to rely on Ms. Skiizer, a 29 year old realtor, to finish the property transaction. For around seven months, she called his residence at least twice a week to update him on her progress. Often time, De'Borah listened to the message on the answer machine as Ms. Skiizer would say, "Isaia, please give me a call concerning a business matter." After copious messages from Ms. Skiizer, De'Borah begins to wonder who is this woman and what did she want from Isaia. The more she reflected on those messages; the more her imagination ran wild, but De'Borah managed to keep her feelings to herself.

More than nine months passed; before Isaia closed on the vacation cottage, when he discovered his business investment with P/Krove En-Vestoe started failing and he lost nearly one hundred twenty thousand dollars. In addition, he knew that De'Borah was getting very suspicious of those telephone messages, and now this financial crisis. Isaia prayed for the courage to tell De'Borah what he'd done with their money. Several more weeks elapsed, before Isaia finally told De'Borah the number of funds they lost from his business venture along with the closing cost of her surprise vacation cottage. "Darling, I didn't want you to find out this way. I wanted…" Interrupting him, De'Borah tearfully said, "You mean to tell me for over ten months you've been hiding this from me? Why, Isaia? What were you thinking? How could you keep something this important from me?" Momentarily a silence filled the room before De'Borah blurted out, "I wonder what else you've been hiding from me."

As their finances deteriorated and their anniversary only six months away, De'Borah and Isaia decided to resign as youth directors of their local church because they couldn't invest the time needed to plan, organize, and put into action activities and programs intended for adolescence . Isaia took a second job that demanded even more of his time; and De'Borah began accumulating a sizeable quantity of overtime. With both of them working extra hours, their eldest child, Jeremas, started falling behind at school. Until one day the principal of Lawn-Gate Private School notified the Sarrmon's that Jeremas will be suspended from school for combated behavior. Without warning, De'Borah felt her stable world crumple around her with no way out. Her nights are sleepless, as she ponders over the thought of what went wrong. On the contrary, Isaia spent many nights contemplating filing for bankruptcy. No one could have told them that their lives will come to this point. To the point where De'Borah, who sat quietly and despondently as Isaia, drove to his parents' house to pick up their children, suddenly could not hold it any longer. De'Borah said the one thing she vowed never to say, **"Isaia, I want a divorce."** Knowing their anniversary is just three weeks away Isaia continued driving speechless, with tears dripping from his cheeks.

THE CHALLENGE

1. After reading the story of Isaia and De'Borah Sarrmon, how do you think their situation could have been handled?

_____

_____

2. In your opinion, what went wrong, or did anything go wrong?

_____

_____

3. If this was my spouse and I, what would or should we do? Would God be pleased with our actions?

_____

_____

Please reconsider your answers after reading this book.

SECTION ONE

Build A Solid Foundation

CHAPTER 1

The Woman's Position

In today's society, women hold many positions of authority. In the United States as well as other countries, a woman can become the president or head of the nation. Women now have the opportunity in America, to seek any position they choose. Nonetheless, when it applies to the home and marriage, her position is documented in the Word of God, the supreme authority on such matters. Those who uphold a secular view of marriage can misconstrue the woman's proper position from a biblical stand point. How she's originally designed and positioned in the Garden of Eden is the key to women discerning their femininity, and how to contend with it.

The Hebrew word for woman is Ishshah (ish-shaw´), which means wife; betrothed one; bride; or just she-man, not associated with the word lesbian, but because she was taken from Man. As stated in Genesis 2: 23 And Adam said: "This is now bone of my bones and flesh of my flesh; she shall be called Woman, because she was taken out of Man." The word Ishshah connotes the femaleness of a woman, with the womb identifying her as absolute female. Ishshah is then reconnected to man through the marriage ceremony conducted by God or more specifically, Jesus. The point is when God presented Ishshah to man; He joined them as one in holy matrimony. Now, woman or Mrs. Adam could help man or Mr. Adam carry out the task (s) that God had assigned him to do. For God had declared, "It is not good that man should be alone; I will make him a helper comparable to him." (Genesis 2: 18)

How God developed man's helper is pivotal to understanding her position as well. After putting him to sleep, God removed a rib from Adam's side and made a helpmeet, that is, a helper like one who is opposite of him, for him. It wasn't by accident that God chose man's rib bone instead of his foot, leg, arm or backbone. As a matter of fact, from a physiological perspective, the place from which He extracted the bone confirms the woman's intended position. Which rib bone God took from Adam isn't specified in the book of Genesis, nor is it vitally important. According to human anatomy, men and women have twelve pairs of ribs or a total of twenty-four ribs. These bones form a cage around the thorax. They give the chest its shape, and protect the vital organs, as well as support the human body. Again, this demonstrates that her position is one of protecting and supporting her husband. Something Eve should have done with Adam in the garden, by encouraging him not to partake of the fruit from the forbidden tree, instead of enticing him with it.

Another point worth mentioning is that the woman, later called Eve isn't created, but drawn from what is in existence (see 1 Timothy 2: 13). Which meant that every human had to derive from one ancestor, the seed of Adam, because if God created Ishshah, then two lines of heredity or federal heads will exist instead of one (see Acts 17: 26 and Romans 9: 21). Hence, every race, kindred, and tongue must trace their roots to either man or woman. But in God's plan for fallen humanity, He made provision for just one redeemer, one death, and one race - humans.

Finally, the word helpmeet is translated from the Hebrew word ezer (ay'-zer) which had two roots that may have derived from the Canaanite/Ugarit language. One of the roots meant to rescue or save, and the other to be strong. One thing for sure, the woman rescued the man or Adam from his inability to procreate upon the earth as he's instructed to do. Adam could not reproduce alone; he needed someone of his likeness, bone of my bones, to produce others with the same likeness. It could only happen with the help of a woman.

Several times in the Old Testament, ezer is associated with military allies. Ally comes from the Latin word alligare meaning to bind to; so, when two or more militaries join forces they become powerful and strong. They can withstand and overcome any opposition or attack from their foes. An ally can be one who sees and knows the enemy. God equipped the woman to be the perfect ally to man. In other words, her duty is to see the foe coming, and to warn her husband that the enemy is going to strike. In doing so, the woman is functioning correctly according to her intended position within the bounds of marriage. Of course, God never intended for her position to be inferior nor superior, but that it will perfectly balance the two of them through wedlock. So when she remains in her rightful position, then it makes her position as equally important as the man's, and the two are stronger together than they are apart.

CHAPTER 2

The Woman's Condition

From the moment God shaped a bone into a woman, she was different from the man. In every way, she's built to support him as anew created man. The woman was, and still is today, suitable for the man. She complements him from every angle and side; whether he is square, rectangular, triangular, oblong, circular, or perpendicular. Whatever the case may be, she is tailored-made to fit him.

After uniting the man and woman, everything was harmonious and peaceful between the couple, until the woman met the serpent and engaged in dialog. At this point, allow me to pause for a moment to say the plan of redemption is released, because something diabolical (no, not sex) happened between the woman and man. It set-off a chain reaction that even affects couples today. It is known as the seed of disobedience or spirit of rebellion. Both the man and woman became a gateway for the seed of disobedience to flourish. Even though both are guilty, but the woman in her condition is used to influence the downfall of her husband. This condition should be meticulously reviewed by today's woman, if she plans to be a virtuous wife.

Notice, the woman is purposefully endowed with intuition,

sometimes called the sixth sense (sorry men, we're stuck with five) since it gives the man sight in more than one direction. Apparently, it's more than her curiosity for the forbidden tree, but her ability to envision them being equal to God, if they partake of its fruit. For this reason, the serpent that's temporarily inhabited by Satan approached the woman because he detected a seed of resentment in her toward the forbidden tree. In essence, she had acquired the spirit of rebellion and presented it to her husband in the Garden of Eden (read Genesis 3: 1-6). So, God had to pronounce judgment upon their disobedience – meaning He set in motion conditions which help correct their deficiency.

(Note: Let's make it plain, God never cursed the man or woman, but the serpent and the ground.)

God's measure of correction is initiated in two vital parts of the woman's life. The first part is with childbearing, where she must endure great physical pain before bringing forth life. Every woman that is impregnated will experience labor pains during the final trimester of her pregnancy. Next, she is judged in her relationship with her husband. In Genesis 3: 16, God said to the woman, "...Your desire shall be for your husband, and he shall rule over you." It does not mean her sexual desire, but in her fallen state, including every woman, she'll try to exercise control over him; but, God gave the husband, including every man, the authority to counter– act the woman trying to master him. This authority that Genesis 3: 16 speaks of is not a new or different charge given to the husband, but the same charge given to Adam in Genesis 2: 15. But due to the fall, his authority now causes competition instead of cooperation. It is a problem in which every martial relationship will encounter sooner or later. But in order for the woman to move forward, she must dissect the nature of Eve to understand how to work inside her home, and do it with the right spirit.

CHAPTER 3

The Woman's Duties

After the woman rebelled and is evicted from the garden, Adam called her Eve, from the Hebrew word chavvah (khav-vaw´) meaning life-giver. Since she is the first human to give birth, hence she was called Eve (see Genesis 3: 20; 4: 1-2). Sadly, many younger women today shun birthing children for a professional career or a carefree life style. In fact, if asked, these women will cite many reasons they should not reproduce. But in spite of this, the fact is, women are built to reproduce and charged by God to help populate the earth with humans. God did not intend for human reproduction to stop at the close of the twentieth century. To stop reproducing means that women are neglecting one of their main duties as it relates to womanhood. In addition to procreating, Eve is commissioned to transform her house into a home. Likewise, every woman born after Eve is bound by the same commission. Just as the man, she has specific duties required of her to make this transformation.

Her first duty is to become a "virtuous wife". Oops! Did I mention that so-called impossible goal to achieve? In fact, many spiritual leaders have liberated their female followers from attempting to become this ideal woman or wife, and most women will shout in unison, with a thunderous - Amen; because their hearts are filled with vanity, pride, sensuality, and the lust for worldly possessions. Nevertheless, every woman should crave and strive to obtain a measure of virtue. It is far better for her to aim for the impossible, than to always settle for mediocrity.

The Bible is the barometer for womanhood, and the book of Proverbs 31: 10-31 lays out the pattern for her life. According to Proverbs 31:10, the woman is to be virtuous or strong. The Hebrew phrase is eshet chayil (khah´ – yil) which means a woman of valor or strength. Her power should flow with the force of a great army. But to have this power or strength, there must be a source whence it comes. The answer is found in Proverbs 31: 30 which state that she is "…a woman who fears the Lord, she shall be praised". In other words, God provides her with a continual flow of power that enables her physically and mentally to fulfill her duties as a "virtuous wife".

Naturally, the man is instructed to search for such virtuous woman. He must pursue her carefully and with extreme attention to details. She is not easily seen, because she is rare and awaiting discovery; but once she is found, her value to him is priceless.

A list of her strong characteristics in Proverbs 31: 10-31 maybe outlined in this manner:

- <u>Fears the Lord:</u> The strongest characteristic of any virtuous wife or woman is to commit herself to the Lord, and have an intimate relationship with Him day by day. To understand His love and inexhaustible resources that He has made available to her; and to know that she is highly favored among the daughters of men.
- <u>Trustworthy:</u> Is when her husband is confident in her willingness to do right in every segment of her life. When her

children know she will tell them the truth, and discipline them when they are wrong, and love them unconditionally.

- <u>Kindhearted toward Husband:</u> She shows a good disposition toward her husband both privately and publicly. As a wife, she wants to always respect her husband even if she doesn't agree with him; because her motive is to do him good the rest of his life.

- <u>A Willing Worker:</u> A woman not afraid to work with her hands or mind whether in the home or outside the home.

- <u>She Rises Early:</u> She arises before day break to prepare things for her husband and children. She does not allow sleepiness to rule over her.

- <u>Prepares Food for Household:</u> In rising early, she prepares a wholesome meal (breakfast) for her family, so they can be nutritiously balanced for their daily activities.

- <u>Entrepreneur:</u> She uses her talent(s) to create a business for the sake of assisting her husband, children, and others that are in need. This woman is not selfish with her profits neither is she consumed with greed.

- <u>Prepares Clothes For Household:</u> Today, lots of women cannot wash/iron clothes, but a virtuous woman is willing to learn and seek-out help. She goes out and purchases her family's clothes and repairs them when needed.

- <u>Hospitable:</u> She is a woman who treats her guest kindly and welcomes them with open arms. She is not afraid to use her fine china-ware and offer them the very best that she posses.

- <u>Holy in Conversation:</u> She chooses her words carefully and seasons them with grace. She doesn't gossip nor does she belittle others, but her conversation is always considerate of others. Her language is never vulgar but is pleasant to hear.

- Keeps Her Home Clean: She understands that cleanliness promotes good health for her family and the environment. By keeping a clean home she will stay in a state of readiness, even if guest should arrive unannounced.
- Prays For Her Home: She is in constant communication with God about her home and the strength she needs to maintain it. She keeps her husband and children before the Lord both day and night.
- Manages Her Time Wisely: A virtuous woman recognize that her time is valuable and she refuses to allow the telephone, television, eateries, shopping malls, or any other things hinder her from her lifelong concern; turning her house into a home that's pleasing to God and her husband.

The basis for these thirteen characteristics is the home. Everything she does is because of her desire to create a home. As a virtuous wife, her life is totally consumed with achieving this task. To desire anything less than this, makes her more voluptuous than virtuous.

CHAPTER 4

The Man's Position

In the day that Adam is created, he's the apex of mankind; the cream of the crop. He is literally, in every sense of the phrase, tall, dark, and handsome. Adam was the human mark of perfection both physically and intellectually. He was flawless. Adam represented humanity, and carried within him the seed of reproduction, not of cloning. In Hebrew, the name Adam (aw-dawm') means man; mankind; people; or to be red, because he is of the dust or reddish soil of the earth as the first man in existence.

As the first man, Adam is placed in a perfect location with an ideal environment. It's a place where his home is an indescribable garden located in the region of Eden. While in the garden, Adam is given five assignments by which he is to govern and supervise the earth. He holds the permanent position of CEO (Chief Executive Officer), and is accountable for what happens in the garden. The five areas assigned to Adam are:

ASSIGNMENT #1:
Procreate the Earth.

This is the first commandment given to Adam by his Creator and a very significant one. It meant that he should reproduce himself, or the image of God upon the earth. Adam had the responsibility of filling the earth with people who had the characteristic or nature of God. Still as a newly created human being, Adam had a major problem that prevented him from completing this assignment. He was single and needed help to fulfill his obligation. God knew just what he needed and formed from him a WOMAN *(Wife)*.

ASSIGNMENT #2:
Subdue the Earth.

Next, God told Adam to subdue the earth. The Hebrew word for subdue is Kabash (kaw-bash´) which means to subject, force, or bring into bondage. But Adam's first command is to fill the earth and then subdue it. So was Adam commanded to enslave his offspring's? Obviously the answer is no. God wanted Adam to take-over where HE had ceased and rested from creation. He should govern the earth as God governs. Yet, God did know that if Adam wasn't obedient, then sin will cause chaos, hostility, violence, decay, and disruption upon the earth. In this instance, Adam must bring things under subjection.

ASSIGNMENT #3:
Dominion Over Animals and the Earth.

Thirdly, Adam will have dominion over the animal kingdom as well as the entire earth. Here, the Hebrew word for dominion is radah (raw-daw´) which means to rule or dominate. After Adam subdued the earth, he'll rule over it, but more importantly is how did God intend for him to rule? Another Hebrew word for dominion is mashal (maw-shal´) which mean liken, or be like.

As a ruler, God intended for Adam to be as HE, and introduce HIM throughout the earth.

ASSIGNMENT #4:
Keeper of the Garden.

Adam's fourth assignment is to keep and protect the garden where he lived. The Hebrew word for keep is shamar (shaw-mar′) and it means to guard, protect, or watch. This assignment made Adam responsible for taking care of the Garden, or his home, because he was physically located there. But in the broader view, Adam represents every man, which makes them the guardians or watchmen over the earth. So as God's representative, Adam is to be aware of what takes place in the garden and throughout the earth, and to make sure that it's done with godliness and in righteousness. Essentially, he was to guard the souls of mankind, but today each man is liable for guarding the souls of his own family.

ASSIGNMENT #5:
Do Not Eat From the Tree of Good & Evil.

The last assignment God gave to Adam was for him not to eat from the Tree of Knowledge of Good and Evil. This made him responsible for informing his wife about God's commandment. As a good husband, Adam stressed to his wife the importance of keeping this commandment. Out-of-each assignment given to Adam, this one determined his eternal position with mankind and in the kingdom of God. Adam should have taken his assignments more serious, as any men should, so God can be truly glorified upon the earth.

God gave Adam the authority to govern and manage the earth in which He had created for mankind. In Psalm 8: 5 the Psalmist writes, "For You have made him a little lower than the angels, And You have crowned him with glory and honor." Adam's paradise was lost when he chose to follow instead of govern as God had instructed him. (See Genesis 1: 28; 2: 7; 2: 15-17)

CHAPTER 5

The Man's Condition

Adam needed to know that he couldn't fulfill his responsibilities alone. He needed a suitable companion to help him execute his duties. Although Adam did not perfectly understand what he needed; after naming the animals, he knew that they could not help him reproduce his own image. Explicitly, Adam's created in the image of God, but missing the feminine human part, requisite for bringing forth humanity. Cause Male + Male = Male not reproduction; Female + Female = Female not reproduction; but Male + Female always equal reproduction. Meanwhile, God addressed his need, by giving him a wife that was capable of satisfying him, and to help carry out his assignments.

As a man, Adam is known as Iysh (eesh), another Hebrew word meaning man or husbandman. Iysh connotes the maleness of Adam, meaning he is absolute male and without female traits. As Iysh, Adam had been joined into a covenant agreement with Ishshah making her his wife. As for the future of marriage, a man must leave his father and mother, and cleave to his wife that they may become one flesh (see Genesis 2: 24). Iysh doesn't waste time in explaining the five assignments to Ishshah in which they are instructed to keep in the garden. Until this point, their home in the garden is filled with tranquility and happiness as they functioned effectively in their perspective positions. But one-day Ishshah had a conversation with one of the animals of the garden regarding the fruit on the Tree of Knowledge of Good and Evil. Even so, her husband wasn't present as she talked to the animal.

(Note: Now various people believe that Iysh was right beside Ishshah as she spoke to the serpent. If this belief is true, then Iysh or Adam is doomed from the day he's created. It meant that Iysh stood in total silence; without conviction; watched and listened to Satan speak through the serpent and deceive Ishshah, and then instantly ate of the fruit himself.)

After eating the fruit herself, she went and offered it to her husband and he without resistance accepted her offer. At this point, he went from hero to zero; from leader to follower; from head to tail, as their condition declined at once and their relationship injured beyond measure. Iysh chose to take part in the rebellion, but in doing so, he forever damaged his home and brought God's judgment upon it. In spite of this, God's judgment is not meant to punish, but to realign their relationship with Him. Another problem Iysh created is chaos within the martial relationship; that is, he'll have to struggle in his marriage to keep control and peace. It's because his wife's desire is to usurp his authority. In Hebrew the word for desire is teshukah, which means to overflow. When something overflows, it completely consumes the thing that holds it. This means she will make an effort to overthrow or dominate her husband even by force if necessary. But in most cases, the woman tries to master the man through manipulation; and manipulation is a form of witchcraft.

Witchcraft is used as a way of controlling the action (s) of another person.

Lastly, before leaving the garden Iysh became an accuser as Satan is an accuser of the brethren. He accused his creator-God, because He gave him the woman, and he accused Ishshah because he listened to her advice. Most husbands today continue to follow the pattern of Iysh- accusing their wives for their mistakes. Men stop accusing your wives as Adam did with his, but speak positive things into her life, so that she can become a woman of excellence.

CHAPTER 6

The Man's Commission

After Adam abdicated his position to govern the world, he infected every man with his inherent weakness. He tried to hide his weakness by accusing God and his wife, instead of admitting he made the wrong decision. Just as Adam, men are still covering up by wearing the mask of Zorro in their relationships, because they are reluctant to put on view their real self. Please! Men it's time to take-off the mask and show your wives your true self including your flaws. Neither spouse can significantly grow as long as they conceal their vulnerability. Unless their weaknesses are exposed, each one will be stagnant and contented.

Let's take under consideration the reputable Zorro, whose name means fox in Spanish. The fox is known for being crafty, when catching its prey. Comparable to Zorro, who in reality is Don Diego Vega, many husbands enjoy being the fox because they want to live double-lives. They want their wives to see them as noble, skillful, and masculine; while secretly they admire another woman or another man, obsessed with pornography, or any other unhealthy sinful habit. Too often, these shameful acts or spiritual strong holds cause many husbands to behave strangely and over react to their wives and family. This will soon become the noose that hangs them.

Often times, Zorro left a distinctive mark on his opponent before fleeing the scene. He purposely etched out the letter "Z" in order for the authorities to know who's responsible for the act. Likewise, a wife receives the last name of her husband when legally married; so when he commits adultery or physically abuses her, then she is left to bear his mark. It's a mark full of pain and humiliation which she has to endure from the court of public opinion. Though, at the end of the original story of Zorro (written by Johnston McCulley in 1919, whose fictional person is of nobility and a skilled swordsman residing in California under Spanish rule) Don Diego Vega removed the mask, which covered his entire face, to uncover the true identity of Zorro. Zorro became extremely popular as a television series in the late 1950's, being portrayed by the actor Guy Williams.

There is an account in the Old Testament from the Book of Zechariah, in which a young man is swiftly making his way to Jerusalem to survey the city (see Zechariah 2: 1-5). In this vision, the prophet Zechariah is speaking with an angel, when he sees a young man running toward Jerusalem. The angel, whom Zechariah is conversing with, dispatches another angel to stop the young man from going to Jerusalem to measure its perimeter; for God did not intend to have walls built around it, because HE wanted to be the protector of the city. It is the same with men today; God doesn't want them to mask their personality, but that they will allow HIM through the Holy Spirit to control their lives and lead them to the whole truth. Thus, God has commissioned or charged every man to carry out his duties that had been assigned to Adam who represented mankind in the Garden of

Eden. As Adam is commissioned to master the Garden of Eden, likewise, every man must first master his own home. This means he must be brazenly honest with himself, family, and God in order for God to effectively use him to reach his household. Then, and only then, will he be ready to master the other areas that God has commissioned him to do.

STOP! LISTEN! CALLING ALL MEN, CALLING ALL MEN: PLEASE REMOVE YOUR MASK!

Praise

PRAISE! What is praise? In Hebrew, many words are used or relates to the term praise *(such as barach, halal, tehillah, gadal, etc.)* but the more familiar usage for praise is **"Yadah"** *(from where the word Judah comes).* The literal meaning of <u>yadah</u> is *to throw or to cast.* So when a husband praises his wife at the gate; he is literally throwing out compliments of her to others. He confesses how much he adores and loves her when he engages in conversation with others. Yet, this praise only happens when she willingly submits to his leadership which should be based on servitude.

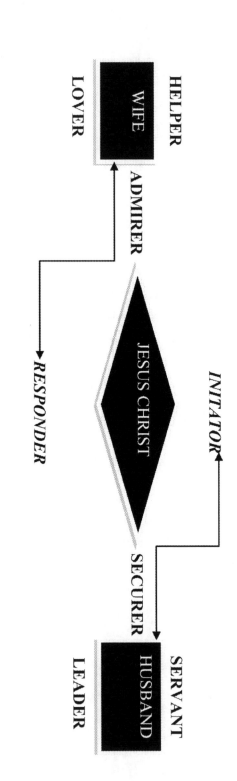

(Diagram 1)

Submission

The words submit tend to make many women cringe or seethe with anger when spoken by most men *(especially, married men)*. This happens because most women associate the term submits with inferiority, slavery, and bondage. The word submits comes from the Greek term **hupotasso** which means <u>hupo</u> *(under)* and <u>tasso</u> *(to arrange)*. Literally, *"to arrange or order oneself under the authority of another."* This means that the woman should be willing to place herself under the headship *(authority)* of her own husband in order for him to lead her and the children. It is true that his leadership should always include his household as a decision-making unit, but he should have the freedom to make the final decision.

SECTION TWO

Relationships Of The Six Kinds

CHAPTER 7

Marriage By Design

> **Abraham/Sarah**
>
> Geographical Location: Canaan
>
> Relation: Husband & Wife
>
> Position: Patriarch & Princess
>
> Marriage Foundation: Solid

SCRIPTURAL WISDOM: *"For in this manner, in former times, the holy women who trusted in God also adorned themselves, being submissive to their own husbands, as Sarah obeyed Abraham, calling him lord, whose daughters you are if you do good and are not afraid with any terror."* (1Peter 3: 5-6)

God intentionally designed the marriage relationship to be a developmental cycle with peaks and valleys, highs and lows that will intimately fuse a husband and wife's personality. So much so, that they began to look, act, and talk the same way. The word design comes from the Latin word designare which means to mark out, designate, or to indicate with a distinctive mark or sign. God plainly offers a strategic approach to arrive at a unique expectation. But to bare this mark of distinction, the relationship must firmly be intact.

As the wife of Abraham, Sarah understood that God's plan was for the two of them to cleave, or to stick as glue together in their relationship. She learned that her part in the relationship equation was to acknowledge the respect she had toward Abraham. Although Sarah was a princess herself, and had traveled close to a thousand miles from Ur her home land with her husband to a land that flowed with milk and honey, she still honored Abraham by calling him lord. In doing this, Sarah became known as a holy woman who trusted God, and the wife who voluntarily put herself beneath her own husband.

But the 21st century woman thinks differently, she diametrically opposes this custom as being antiquated and unsound. The modern woman prefers equality over submission, and believes by replacing the man with a more aggressive woman in the home will create a stronger relationship. She proclaims that Sarah misunderstood the plan, because God never insist on this behavior whether pass or present. The woman is just as equal as the man in the marital relationship.

In accordance with Christian egalitarianism, meaning equal responsibility, headship/authority; marriage is a full partnership with no differentiation between headships. Their roles are gift-based as oppose to gender-based. But even if true, what happens when husband/wife can't reach an agreement or compromise on a precarious matter? Someone must make that final decision-God chose man!! It is the positional roles that God designed to make the relationship work smoothly. Balance is reached when those within the relationship serve one hundred percent in their own position. Since Sarah operated in her position, in return, Abraham trusted her judgment, praised her wisdom and attractiveness, shared his authority and mourned at her passing (see Genesis 23: 2). By putting Abraham in his rightful position, Sarah received the boundless love of her husband.

More often than not, for most people relationship is purely a word with very little meaning to the ones involved. But, a closer examination of the word relationship may well hold the key to achieving oneness. When the word relationship is divided into syllables it means:

- *Re:* back to the original place, again and again.
- *Relate:* from Latin relatus (or referre) = to carry back.
- *ion:* act of process (the result of).
- *ship:* from old English scieppan = to shape.

In a relationship, each person must return to the original plan or God's design again and again to shape the outcome of the marriage. As a potter who returns to the clay and constantly molds and shapes it into a masterful piece of art. So husbands must return to their position, one of authority, and fashion their position to resemble God's plan of authority. As for wives, to truly be the daughters of Sarah they must return to a position of submission, because it matches God's plan for their marriage.

CHAPTER 8

Marriage By Partiality

Isaac/Rebekah

Geographical Location: Negev/South Canaan

Relation: Husband & Wife

Position: Wealthy Farmer/Herdsman/Patriarch

Marriage Foundation: Firm

SCRIPTURAL WISDOM: *So the boys grew. And Esau was a skillful hunter, a man of the field; but Jacob was a mild man, dwelling in tents. And Isaac loved Esau because he ate of his game, but Rebekah loved Jacob. (Genesis 25: 27-28)*

Love–at–first–sight is how Isaac and Rebekah began their relationship. Isaac, who was deeply depressed due to the death of his mother Sarah, is comforted after marrying Rebekah and taking her into his mother's tent (Gen. 24: 67). As his wife, Rebekah reminded Isaac of the woman Sarah had been to him and his father Abraham. Most men are inclined to choose a woman who has the same qualities or characteristics as their mother, to be their wife. Even if those qualities in their mother are wicked and demonic.

Twenty years was the length of time Isaac and Rebekah had, because of her barrenness; to strengthen and develop their relationship, but instead, they became more and more isolated as time passed. Each one had gradually slid into their own world where they found consolation for themselves. But the day came when Isaac entreated the Lord to fertilize Rebekah's womb that she may bare children. God answered Isaac's prayer, for twins emerged from the struggle of Rebekah's pregnancy with the youngest one's hand gripping the heel of the elder. It was a sign that the younger son Jacob will prevail over the elder son Esau.

As the twins grew into manhood, the parents favored their sons, Isaac to Esau, Rebekah to Jacob. Later on, this favoritism drove Rebekah to deceive her husband Isaac, despite his blindness, and to overlook her elder son Esau. But in particular, it caused her to lose whom she loved most – Jacob.

Partiality in any marriage leads to an unbalanced relationship no matter who's involved. The word partiality means "one – sidedness." In the case of Isaac and Rebekah, each one leaned toward what they admired most in their sons, instead of rearing them together as a family unit. It harmed their marriage in a way that they never felt the oneness God affirms in a marriage. The thing's partiality cost them were:

- Father/Son relationship (Isaac/Jacob)
- Mother/Son relationship (Rebekah/Esau)
- Trust between husband/wife
- Regular intimacy between husband/wife
- Lucid /healthy communication between family members

- Sibling rivalry (Esau/Jacob)
- A close-knit family (parents/children)

To try to build a relationship through favoritism will always have a negative outcome to one degree or another. As for Rebekah and Isaac, their relationship didn't advance beyond the point it was before they had children. Their marriage started with the hope that love can weave them closer together, but their proclivity toward partiality held them in suspended animation and the sons were the padlock that prevented any movement. However, the real answer was for them to favor each other as married people should, and to focus on raising their children in the admonition of the Lord.

CHAPTER 9

No Marriage By Infatuation

Amnon/Tamar

Geographical Location: Jerusalem

Relation: Incestuous

Position: Prince/Princess

No Marriage Foundation

SCRIPTURAL WISDOM: *"And I, where could I take my shame? And as for you, you would be like one of the fools in Israel. Now therefore, please speak to the king; for he will not withhold me from you." However, he would not heed her voice; and being stronger than she, he forced her and lay with her. Then Amnon hated her exceedingly, so that the hatred with which he hated her was greater than the love with which he had loved her. And Amnon said to her, "Arise, be gone!"* (II Samuel 13: 13-15)

Why are men bedazzled by what they think is love? A love smeared with romantic imagery of the woman in whom they believe is the one, that special one. They believe this tarnished love entitles them to the person they see as being set aside just for them, and whatever it takes to soothe this passionate love they will embrace it. Such was the case of Amnon and Tamar.

In the biblical story, Princess Tamar, daughter of King David, showed the physical signs of puberty (between 10-15 years of age) that soon caught the attention of Prince Amnon. Amnon was the eldest son of King David, half-brother of Tamar, and next in line for the throne. He found himself obsessed with his young sister's cuteness to the point that he could not discharge her from his mind, and felt he had to have her. After discussing his obsession with his clever acquaintance Jonadab, whom the bible says was Amnon's cousin; Jonadab concocted a plan that will put Amnon alone with Tamar. Under the pretext of being sick, Amnon convinced his father King David to allow the Princess to come to his private quarters to cook a meal for him. The King agreed, and Tamar after leaving the safety of her royal harem is lured into the bedroom of Amnon where he committed the sin of rape. How can Amnon commit such horrific act on the person whom he loved?

The word love come from the old English word léof meaning "dear" or to hold a person dear, and to consider that person precious. Amnon did not consider Tamar to be precious because he utterly destroyed her after claiming he loved her. What's more his so-called love disintegrated into hatred the moment he finished his brutal assault on the object of his affection-Tamar.

This behavior doesn't match a person who is truly in love, but in a similar way it fit a person who is infatuated with another. Infatuate can be linked to the Latin word infatuare which means "to make a fool of" or to become foolish. Amnon made a fool of himself by behaving as an animal who acts impulsively and disorderly. The same as a thief, he stole Tamar's virginity and robbed her of a meaningful life.

Even so, sin never goes unpunished, whether in this life or the life to come, but for Amnon it came two years later. Tamar's brother Absalom set a trap for Amnon and ordered his servants to stab him to death at a feast he gave for the sons of David. But Tamar is still condemned to a life of shame, loneliness, and tormented from the scars of an incestuous violation. Following this callous act, Amnon refused to marry her after violating her body, and the bible never mentions that Tamar ever married.

Infatuation usually doesn't lead to marriage, but when it does, the marriage is doomed to fail. As one can see in this story, infatuation can lead to obsession, and obsession may lead to rape. In Tamar's case, she paid a terrible price for the sins of her father King David; because the house of David is under a curse for his adultery with Bathsheba and the murder of her husband Uriah (see Second Samuel 12: 9-12). This is one reason parents shouldn't break their marriage vow, because it can affect the lives of their children and even their children's children. Granted Tamar's name means palm tree which typifies food, security, and life yet, she lost that security and lived a desolated life.

CHAPTER 10

Marriage By Arrangement

> ### Nabal/Abigail
>
> Geographical Location: Maon/Judah
>
> Relation: Husband/Wife
>
> Position: Wealthy Herdsman (sheep/goats)
>
> Marriage Foundation: Weak

SCRIPTURAL WISDOM: *Now there was a man in Maon whose business was in Carmel, and the man was very rich. He had three thousand sheep and a thousand goats. And he was shearing his sheep in Carmel. The name of the man was Nabal, and the name of his wife Abigail. And she was a woman of good understanding and beautiful appearance; but the man was harsh and evil in his doings. And he was of the house of Caleb. (1 Samuel 25: 2-3)*

Sometimes a few marriages are made in heaven, while others are made by those who believe they know what's best for someone else. This is precisely what happened with the union of Abigail and Nabal. More than likely, Abigail's father had arranged the marriage between her and Nabal, because he's a very rich man with enough wealth for his daughter, Abigail, and himself. Still today, cultures of South Asia, East Asia, Africa, and the Middle East practice arranging marriages. The Hebrew term for such marriage is shadkhan which means "to arrange a marriage" or "matchmaker". Those who are shadkhanims, even if they are trained professionals; usually they're compensated with a percentage of the dowry, and by charging other fees as well. It was a lucrative occupation then, as well as now. In fact, Abigail's father disregarded the flawed nature of Nabal, in which he most likely foreknew while approving their marrying; but the lust for riches and fame causes many to deny the truth, and risk the happiness of others for self-gratification.

The disposition of Nabal (naw-bawl') is tied directly to his name which meant fool, foolish, or vile person. As a vile person, he's often harsh and unfair in both his public and private life. Even as a businessman, Nabal's a brute and scoundrel who maliciously rebuffed those messengers of David sent to bless him. Men such as Nabal are usually disrespectful to those around them, including their wife and children, and are morally bankrupt. Often time they will inebriate themselves and become much more villainous; making them unbearable to live with under the same roof. He is an arrogant rich selfish individual who thought that others should adhere to his demands. The eleventh verse of First Samuel 25 bears witness to this fact when Nabal answered David's servants saying, "Shall I then take my bread and my water and my meat that I have killed for my shearers, and give it to men when I do not know where they are from?" Seven times he refers to himself, and the number seven means complete; in reality Nabal is completely selfish, and a selfish husband never puts his wife first.

Abigail knows she's miss-matched with a tyrant, but as a wife of good understanding she managed to honor him as best as she could given her circumstance. Many women are unequally yoked to men who have become their worst nightmare and their only wish is to break away or separate themselves from their spouse. They see their relationship as irreparable and divorce as the only alternative. But in Abigail's case, she chose to stay married and trusted God to work out her state of affairs. She did not harbor bitterness or anger toward her husband, but she acted as a mediator or conciliator on his behalf. As the Apostle Paul said in his letter to the Corinthians, "For the unbelieving husband is sanctified by the wife, and the unbelieving wife is sanctified by the husband; otherwise your children would be unclean, but now they are holy." (1 Corinthians 7: 14)

As a believer, Abigail will not ask God to kill Nabal but to save him. Yet, Nabal's recklessness arose before God and he became viciously ill for ten days; then died of apoplexy. Bear in mind, every unscrupulous marriage will not end with the death of a spouse, but God can change the condition if HE wants to through righteousness. Nothing's wrong with matching people together, but to match the wrong ones is sinful. God and not the internet is the greatest matchmaker, so why not let HIM introduce you to your spouse.

CHAPTER 11

Marriage By Compatibility

Ahab/Jezebel

Geographical Location: Samaria

Relation: Husband/Wife

Position: King/Queen

Marriage Foundation: Stable/Deceptive

SCRIPTURAL WISDOM: *So Ahab went into his house sullen and displeased because of the word which Naboth the Jezreelite had spoken to him; for he said, "I will not give you the inheritance of my fathers." And he lay down on his bed, and turned away his face, and would eat no food. But Jezebel his wife came to him, and said to him, "why is your spirit so sullen that you eat no food?" So he said to her, "Because I spoke to Naboth the Jezreelite, and said to him, "Give me your vineyard for money; or else, if it pleases you, I will give you another vineyard for it." And he answered, 'I will not give you my vineyard.' Then Jezebel his wife said to him, "You now exercise authority over Israel! Arise and eat food, and let your heart be cheerful; I will give you the vineyard of Naboth the Jezreelite." (1 Kings 21: 4 – 7)*

One of the most intriguing couples recorded in the Bible was Ahab and Jezebel. Ahab ruled the Northern Kingdom of Israel for twenty – two years. He is the seventh King of Israel who inherited the Kingdom from his father Omri. The seat of his power is located in Samaria, the capital of Northern Israel. Under Ahab, several cities were fortified to protect the citizens from military assaults by neighboring countries. He's able to negotiate successful trade agreements with merchants in the northern parts of Canaan. Ahab used his military might to strengthen and secure peace in the region as he formed alliances with other nations. These alliances are commonly sealed by marriages and/or religion. It was politically wise for Ahab's father to arrange a future marriage between him and Jezebel, the daughter of the king of Tyre. By doing this, Israel and Tyre will no longer be enemies but allies.

As a King, Ahab reigned with power and might, but as a husband he's a very poor example to follow. On one hand, he shows great courage in conquering his enemies; but morally he is a weak man who yearns for the wealth and luxuries of this world. Due to his moral weakness, his wife Jezebel becomes the voice and vigor of morality in Northern Israel.

When Ahab brought his young Phoenician/Tyrian bride to her new palace in Samaria, she came with an agenda. As the new Queen, her ploy is to dominate her husband as well as the nation. Jezebel's well prepared by her father Ethbaal who had murdered his brother for the throne of Tyre, and an ardent worshiper of Baal, the Canaanite deity of nature and fertility. Many believed that Baal had the power to tame the weather and give or withhold a woman's fertility. These customs and beliefs is what Jezebel came with into Samaria to impose upon her husband and many other Israelites, who suppose to believe in a monotheistic God, the creator of every thing. She's so domineering that she before long becomes the master of her husband, Ahab. Soon Temples are built in Israel to worship Baal and Asherah, the goddess of love, and prostitutes who's eager to lure the people into mendacity. Inwardly, Ahab knew this was the wrong path to follow; still he sanctioned her religion; which was more of a cult than a religion, where it summarily bloomed in Northern Israel.

In the tenacious grasp of a strong-willed woman as Jezebel, Ahab adopted the role of a son in lieu of a king. This shatter proofed their relationship which turns out to be more of a mother-son in contrast to a King-Queen relationship. Women who mimic Jezebel see their husband as an underdeveloped man with childish behavior, and in need of a mother to maneuver him in the way he should go. Ahab's silent resentment toward Naboth's refusal to give up his land infuriated Jezebel and authorized her conduct with her husband. In the end, it led her to conspire to have Naboth murdered, then take over his land and give it to her husband as a gift. Any man, who accepts such a gift, makes him compatible to his wife. In Ahab's case, he agreed with his wife's action and showed no remorse for what happened to Naboth. People whose persona epitomizes Ahab and Jezebel should not be wedded together, because it will end in disaster if neither one changes.

CHAPTER 12

Marriage By Possession

Ananias/Sapphira

Geographical Location: Jerusalem

Relation: Husband/Wife

Position: Land Owners

Marriage Foundation: Firm

SCRIPTURAL WISDOM: *But a certain man named Ananias, with Sapphira his wife, sold a possession. And he kept back part of the proceeds, his wife also being aware of it, and brought a certain part and laid it at the apostles' feet. (Acts 5: 1-2)*

Jesus had physically come and gone when the early Church opened its doors. By now it's known as the Church of Jerusalem, and the Apostle Peter is chosen to lead these new followers of Christ. They hastily become a kibbutz of believers who voluntarily share their wealth with each other. Those who owned land or houses freely sold it, and laid the proceeds at the apostles' feet. Anyone with a need amid this body of believers, the apostles allocated a section to them. Undeniably, the church grew from the apostles' fidelity and steadfastness to Christ; to having everything in common.

Into this predominantly Jewish church environment, came Ananias and his wife Sapphira. They entered a church where love, peace, gentleness, long-suffering, and the outpouring of the Holy Spirit are preeminent. As young Christ-followers with five thousand new converts, they spoke the word of God boldly (See Acts 4: 31).These followers of Christ are a beacon of light in the city of Jerusalem and was spreading it to other parts of the middle-east. Their generosity is unparalleled and acquired the attention of Ananias and Sapphira. Yet it wasn't the generosity that drew them, but the accolades they stood to gain from it. They wanted the same recognition the church gave to Barnabas, a name that means the son of consolation; to be bestowed upon them, minus the generous gifts Barnabas had donated to the church. It is ironic how the name Ananias being imported from the Hebrew word chananiyah meaning the "grace or mercy of the Lord", and the name Sapphira meaning "beautiful"; ultimately resulted in shame and disgrace. God graciously blessed this couple with health, wealth, and beauty; still they chose the path to greed than to generosity.

As a wife, Sapphira should have tried to attract Ananias to doing what's right with the money he received from selling the land; instead she became an accomplice to withholding part of the profit and may have instigated it herself. For what one possesses often has a way of corrupting them when they see it as the answer to life's problems. But in reality they have the answer, God the one who draws them with His Holy Spirit. The same Holy Spirit that drew them to God shined that eternal light upon their hearts to make known to the church their true intentions. They are welded by their possessions and acted as one, but this unity comes with an awful price. The price is death. What the two of them coveted is noble, but the way they wanted to secure that status, is without exception wrong. Truth is, the only thing they possessed is their soul, and even it belonged to God. Just as others, they too stood before the apostles and agreed to give the entire proceeds to the early church; so God held them to that agreement; HE asked for their lives! No husband and wife should be so close that they are willing to tell the same lie to God for material gain and undeserved recognition.

CHAPTER 13

Money Does Matter (In Today's Relationships)

In today's world, where people appear to be wiser and thriftier, they're more concern for their checking and saving accounts, than their integrity. The normal fad is for women to pursue men with a six figure income ($100,000 plus) or something in that vicinity. At the same time, men will choose women who are unattached and have many material possessions; or women who are single parents with genuine stability and sleek transportation. Regardless of the circumstances, a person's source of income is a major issue in most relationships. Should money matter? Should one's level of income decide who will become their spouse? These are two very important questions, because thousands of marriages are dissolved over the issue of money. Fact is many people are opting out of their marriage because they are overloaded with debt. But to reach a sound conclusion on the topic of money, one must understand the basis of money and how prominent money is according to the Bible.

The word money is believed to have derived from the Latin word monere meaning to remind, warn, or instruct. In ancient

Rome, a temple's erected in honor of the mythical goddess, Juno; supposedly she had alerted the Roman soldiers of an oncoming attack launched by their enemy. This early warning allowed the Roman soldiers to defeat their opposition. To show their appreciation toward her, they named the temple Juno Moneta. At this temple, which stood on the Capitoline Hill of Rome, the Romans minted bronze and silver coins for circulation. These coins are called Moneta, a title given to the goddess Juno, from where we get our English terms money, monetize, and mint. The coins became the method by which the Romans used as a medium of exchange for goods and services rendered. Centuries later, Rome virtually replaced the coins with high value paper notes for money.

In the United States, paper money is a note-a Federal Reserve Note. This paper money is called fiat currency, meaning it has no inherent value. These notes are produced by the U.S. Treasury, through its Bureau of the Mint and Bureau of Engraving/ Printing; then sold to the Federal Reserve Banks at manufacturing cost. The Federal Reserve Banks then distribute the coins and paper currency to other financial institutions stationed throughout the United States. Once the Federal Reserve Notes are put into circulation, they become the responsibility of the U.S. Government. It's a sign that the U.S. Government is primarily the source or maker behind the note. Hence, if the government fails the Federal Reserve Note is useless. With this being true, why then are multiple people perishing and relationships torn apart for something that has no value? When undoubtedly, the Bible describes how we should measure money and how we are presumed to manage it.

The Bible addresses money extensively in the areas of investing, saving, lending, borrowing, spending, and tithing. It shows the stress God puts on the way we handle our money comparative to our relationship with Him. If we become too preoccupied with making money, then our relationship with God will drift away, as it will with our husband or wife or any close relationship. In the Gospel of Matthew 6: 19-21 is written, "Do not lay up for yourselves treasures on earth, where moth and rust destroy and where thieves break in and steal; but lay up for yourselves treasures in heaven, where neither moth nor rust destroys and where thieves do not break in and steal. For where your treasure is, there your heart will be also." As for those who place a very high value on money, they may be offended by this passage of scriptures, and view them as diminishing the importance of money or income needed to meet our daily needs. God knows our needs and He wants to supply them daily. He never advised us not to earn money for meeting our obligations such as, paying our debts. Nevertheless, God is very displeased when we substitute our relationship with Him for a higher salary and a more prestigious position. This is why Matthew reminds us of what Jesus said, "Therefore do not worry, saying, 'What shall we eat?' or 'What shall we drink?' or 'What shall we wear?' For after all these things the Gentiles seek. For your heavenly Father knows that you need all these things. But seek first the kingdom of God and His righteousness, and all these things shall be added to you." (Matt. 6: 31-33)

Now for our sake, God doesn't ask for every minute of our time, money, and possessions but demands only a small percentage; ten percent, and that we give it first. Ironically though, the more we love God; the more time, money, and possessions we'll give HIM. The same principle applies to our spouses; the more we love them, then the more time we want to spend with them.

So, as long as we categorize money correctly, and use it prudently, it will be a useful tool in our marriage and our kingdom journey.

The 5 Don'ts about Money

- Don't Love Money
- Don't Covet Money
- Don't Waste Money
- Don't Steal Money
- Don't Live For Money

MONEY MATTERS {Examples}

Most families throughout the world have problems when it comes to money; either there's not enough or it's miss-managed by the one (s) in charge. Besides, money is one of the contributing factors to the divorce rate. Here are two **family formulas** you can solve to see which family makes the most, saves the most, and the most left after each deduction. Do joining family incomes together alter what a family spends and saves? **Remember it's the gross summation of the joint income per family with each member working @ 40-hours per week. Before any bills are paid, tithes/offering deducted first, followed by your savings deduction. But to get a more realistic income total, one may subtract the general deductions/add more household expenses or use their own income/pay checks.**

FAMILY FORMULA (1)

Household Income: Annually_____

Monthly_____

- Father: 50 yrs. Old= $12.50 per hour
- Mother: 53 yrs. Old= $9.00 per hour
- Sister: 24 yrs. Old= $7.25 per hour
- Sister: 18 yrs. Old= $7.25 per hour
- Brother: 20 yrs. Old= $7.25 per hour
- *Savings= 8% monthly deposited into saving account (each family member agree to the percentage and to participate)*

HOUSEHOLD EXPENSES MONTHLY

Tithes $_____ / Offering **$85.00** (monthly)

Mortgage= **$795.00**

Lights/Water= **$285.00**

Telephone= **$260.00**

Groceries= **$825.00**

Transportation (fuel/insurance) = **$1,025.00**

TOTAL MONTHLY INCOME *AFTER* EXPENSES=

_____

TOTAL MONTHLY/YEARLY SAVING (@ 8% X 12) =

_____

FAMILY FORMULA (2)

Household   Income: Annually_____
Monthly_____

- Father: 38 yrs. Old= $28.00 per hour
- Mother: 31 yrs. Old= $16.50 per hour
- Son: 10 yrs. Old= $0.00 per hour
- Savings= 10% monthly deposited into saving account

HOUSEHOLD EXPENSES MONTHLY

Tithes $_____/ Offering **$150.00** (monthly)

Mortgage= **$1,500.00**

Lights/Water= **$375.00**

Telephone= **$175.00**

Groceries= **$695.00**

Transportation (fuel/insurance) = **$585.00**

TOTAL MONTHLY INCOME AFTER EXPENSES =
_____

TOTAL MONTHLY/YEARLY SAVING (@ 10% X 12) =
_____

SECTION THREE

Communication
Liberation
Unification

CHAPTER 14

Forever Talking: What's In a Word?

SCRIPTURAL WISDOM: Ephesians 5: 4 teaches us that our language should not be, "neither filthiness, nor foolish talking, nor coarse jesting, which are not fitting, but rather giving of thanks."

Some people think that words are just words when they are doing the talking. It never occurs to them that whenever problems between two individuals arise, it can usually be traced to the way they communicate or don't communicate. If true, then every individual should choose their words wisely, so that they may provoke the most adequate reaction from the other party. For in the final analysis, how each individual interprets those words spoken to them will decide the response one renders.

There is a cliché that say, "Sticks and stones may break my bones, but words will never hurt me." Unfortunately, the truth is words can emotionally destroy a person even to the point of committing suicide. The book of Proverbs say, "You are snared by the words of your own mouth; You are taken by the words of your mouth." (Proverbs 6: 2) What we say out of anger or frustration, not only harm others, but can entangle us. One word spoken out-of-season can take a lifetime to regain; so that one word should never be spoken. In most relationships at least two behaviors are displayed: the dominator and the submitter. These behaviors can cripple the progress of communicating with one another, if the individuals especially, husbands and wives don't understand the distinction between their roles and how they are to communicate. So clarifying these terms, a person's role is the part they play in the relationship; while communication is how they relate to and understand one another. But in communication, there must be mutual submission or what may be called a courtesy card, and it's imperative that we use this courtesy card in our conversations. In layman's term, it means the sender becomes the receiver and the receiver becomes the sender, or I listen to you and you listen to me. By swiping your courtesy card in the relationship, it dismisses the aspiration for one to dominate the other. Each should always be courteous and mutually surrender to one another to decode their message (s) accurately.

YOUR
COURTESY
CARD

Always Keep It With You

So in spite of theories, patterns, and models rationalizing the success or failure in interpersonal communication; it's God who places serious emphasis upon the need to listen. In Deuteronomy 6: 4-5 the LORD said, "Hear, O Israel: The LORD our God, the LORD is one! You shall love the LORD your God with all your heart, with all your soul, and with all your might." These words are so powerful that members of the Jewish faith will recite verse four at least twice a day. This is called The Shema: "Hear, O Israel: The Lord our God is one Lord." God isn't just speaking to the Jews, but every race should give their utmost attention to such an important matter. He is saying to each of us, "Hear, O <u>Your Name</u>," what I'M going to tell you. Well if listening is exceptionally important to God, then couples should make it a top priority in their conversations? Talking to each other should never cease in the relationship, and practicing the art of listening will make nearly everyone of your disagreements fade away.

REMEMBER! STOP! LOOK! LISTEN!

CHAPTER 15

The Mouth Trap

We must admit that the tongue is a small member of the body when compared to the hand, forearm, or thigh. But it can speak as a giant and kill a person's spirit with just one word. In the epistle of James 3: 5, it says that "Even so the tongue is a little member and boasts great things. See how great a forest a little fire kindles!" Yet, the tongue is basically made of skeletal muscle without bones and a primary blood supply from the lingual artery. It is primarily used for human communication, with the average adult size tongue being 6.5 centimeters long. Presently, according to the Guinness World Records 2009 book, a man from the United Kingdom has the longest tongue reported to be 3.86 inches long; and a U.S woman with the tongue length of 3.8 inches in September of 2010. The Latin word for tongue is lingua, and there are at least two words in English that stems from it, that is language and linguistic. Literally, in most countries, their word for language has a basic root that means the mother tongue. As a result, what we say is very important when it comes to communicating with each other. The book of Proverbs 15: 1-2 puts it this way, "A soft answer turns away wrath, but a harsh word stirs up anger. The tongue of the wise uses knowledge rightly, but the mouth of fools pours forth foolishness." No doubt, the sharpness of a wagging tongue has unraveled the self-esteem of many husbands, wives, and children.

Although anyone can speak harshly out of anger, but most women are endowed with a special ability in utilizing their tongue. Sorry to say, too many of them choose to use this ability in a negative and demeaning way. Whether they're North Americans, South Americans, Europeans, Africans, Asians, Australians, or any other race; their tongue has caused so many homes to become dysfunctional and disconnected, because they have used it as a battering ram on their husbands and children. Men will, if not careful, use their tongue in the same destructive way as the woman. It often becomes a progressive and vicious cycle that perpetuates itself through several generations.

At last, in trying to confirm how destructive the tongue can be, allow me to recount a section of the biblical story of Samson and Delilah (see Judges 16: 15-17). By this time, Samson had lost his Philistine wife, and slew a thousand Philistine soldiers with the fresh jawbone of a donkey. He had slept with a Philistine prostitute, and walked away with the huge gates to the city of Gaza. Until finally, Samson fell in love with another Philistine woman he singled out in the Valley of Sorek only a few miles from Samson's hometown of Zorah where they possibly met by a brook in the valley. Wherever he met this woman her name is Delilah and she interrogated him on his clandestine strength. The name Delilah has connections to the word dalal, (daw-lal′) which means to slacken or be feeble. She intended to weaken Samson with her gorgeousness and treachery. Upon each visit, Samson tease or lie to her as to how she could make him as weak as any other man. After Samson played the cat and mouse game for the third time, Delilah took a different approach in the way she spoke to him. She was adamant in discovering the secret of his strength, because the leaders of the Philistines had promised to pay her eleven hundred pieces of silver if she could help capture Samson. There were five rulers over the Philistine nation because the region had five major cities: Ashkelon, Ashdod, Ekron, Gath, and Gaza (See Joshua 3: 13). These pieces of silver offered to Delilah by the Philistine rulers were a total of 5,500 shekels that valued over fifty thousand dollars.

The Bible says that she began to pester him daily with her words. She nagged him day after day until his soul's vexed; until he felt as though he was going to die. In addition to pestering him, Delilah pressed him. The Hebrew word for press means to oppress, or to be an oppressor. In this case, Delilah became an oppressor for the demise of Samson. Furthermore, the Hebrew word for vexed is qatsar which means to discourage, grieve or to cut down. In other words, Delilah slashed him down so much with her tongue to he became very discouraged and grieved so that he willingly told the truth as to the origin of his strength. Just as Delilah, many women (especially wives) have used this same tactic to get what they want from their husbands. So wives beware of an uncontrolled tongue, it can ravage your home; and let not your mouth be a trap, but let it be the instrument for declaring good tidings and great joy in your home.

CHAPTER 16

Forgive To Live

Indubitable forgiveness is not remembering past offenses, when God Himself has promised as to our iniquities, He will remember no more-if we ask to be forgiven.

As a jigsaw puzzle with various pieces that fit perfectly together, so is a successful marriage when joined with the right ingredients such as love, patience, kindness, meekness, trustworthiness and commitment. Yet, to remove either of these ingredients can disrupt the harmony and success of a marriage, and kill its longevity. Nonetheless, another key ingredient that so many couples neglect to mix with these other ingredients, because of what it entails them to do. This ingredient will rebuild and restore over time, a broken relationship if given a chance. The ingredient is called forgiveness. The word forgive is translated into old English as the word forgiefan from the Latin word perdonare, per meaning thoroughly and donare meaning to give up, to forgive. So in essence, to forgive one's spouse is to do it thoroughly or completely, and without hesitation. It's refusing the right to be angry, resentful, or bitter

J. Martin

towards the one who offended you. No marriage can be successful or long-lived when a couple is unwilling to forgive each other. Even if they choose to stay married without this ingredient, they will just exist under the same roof.

Forgiveness is something many couples find extremely difficult to activate, especially, when one spouse feels as though the ill-act of the other is too offensive. For this reason, the victimized spouse feels justified in their resentment toward their mate, until they gain a sense of satisfaction; regardless of how much mental and physical anguish it causes the guilty spouse. Their aim is to make the guilty one suffer enough until it eases the pain of the innocent one. But forgiveness shouts out to the innocent party, "let it go!" In doing so, the husband or wife who let go of their ideas, views, and opinions of the circumstance and their mate; must put themselves in the same position as the one who committed the violation. Then by placing themselves in that position; they can decide whether the guilty one needs justice or mercy. At this crucial moment, their decision will liberate or incarcerate them.

Basically, forgiveness is akin to climbing a mountain in which every husband and wife should strive to reach its peak. But to get to that point, they must have the proper gear to be able to handle the rocky terrain, increasing height, massive width, and unpredictable weather on the mountain. Because when climbing MT. PERDONARE, a person will come upon various altitudes before reaching the highest elevation. These are the six (6) elevations that form MT. PERDONARE:

ELEVATION #1: Reverse Anger – renew your mind, to take a fresh out-look at the end results of your circumstance. Learn to renew your thoughts. Too much anger will sooner or later kill you. So reverse the spelling of anger and add a few letters of your own.

(r e g _ n _ _ a _ _ / Hint: spiritually reborn)

ELEVATION #2: Refocus your Vision – mentally revisit your affair and seek out those things that have adversely affected your spouse. You will see what you didn't see the first time.

ELEVATION #3: The Judas Factor – Judas Iscariot is known for his betrayal of Jesus along with the thirty pieces of silver he earned from the Jewish leaders, but lots of people have betrayed Jesus freely. Have you ever betrayed anyone?

ELEVATION #4: Reverse Role – Try placing yourself in the same situation as your spouse, under the same condition(s), and with the same frame of mind. Will your response be the same, similar, or totally different?

ELEVATION #5: Mercy Beget Mercy – When an individual is merciful, then they are at liberty to receive mercy. The Bible says, *"Blessed are the merciful, for they shall obtain mercy."* (Matthew 5: 7)

ELEVATION #6: Limitless Love – Real love knows no boundaries and will emancipate you from bitterness, hatred, and jealousy. It will launch you to the peak of the mountain. Those who are exhausted, broken, weak, thirsty, and falls into the arms of Jesus with complete confidence in Him are the only ones who reach this level.

MT. PERDONARE

Limitless Love

Mercy Beget Mercy

Reverse Role

The Judas Factor

Refocus Your Vision

Reverse Anger

Climb Your Mountain to Its Peak (Diagram 2)

CHAPTER 17

Intimacy: The Sacred Bedroom

"Marriage is honorable among all, and the bed undefiled; but fornicators and adulterers God will judge." (Hebrews 13: 4)

How sacred is your bedroom? On a scale of one-to-ten, where do you rate your bedroom? Before you can answer these questions, you must first comprehend the meaning of sacred. It is from the Latin word sacrare, which means to set apart, consecrate or reserve for a person or thing. Here, it refers to a room specifically set apart for the activities of a husband and wife. With marriage being a sacred union, so should your bedroom be as well, because the bedroom's an intrinsic part of the marital relationship.

Every bedroom should be a place of privacy and not defiled by unacceptable behavior. Moreover, couples need to compel themselves to making their bedroom sacred enough to have a sense of oneness when they retreat to it for rest, relaxation, or pleasure whether in the morning, noon, or night. Keep in mind that other people including your own children, will not treat your bedroom as a consecrated room; nor will they respect it as a hallow place. In fact, God has commanded us to keep the bedroom sacred according to Hebrews 13: 4, "Marriage is honorable among all, and the bed undefiled; but fornicators and adulterers God will judge."

Many people take this passage of scripture to mean that everything is permissible as long as they are legally married. This reminds me of a couple on a television talk show, who with child – like enthusiasm said, "Anything goes in our bedroom!" They meant it literally and wanted the audience to know it as well. In the same way, God has given His commandment for us to uphold the sacredness of marriage from the chapel to the bedroom. He has declared in Hebrews 13: 4 what will happen when the bed is debased by acts of ungodliness. This is not a threat from God, but an unmitigated promise; because sexually perverted behavior is strictly prohibited in the bedroom whether it comes from the husband or wife; from a saint or a sinner. These aberrant sexual practices are dangerous, and will indeed manufacture an unhealthy intimate relationship.

Usually, sexual perverted behaviors are not just habits that can be controlled by resistance, but they are deep – seated problems which can lead to hospitalization or death. Technically, Psychologists will diagnosis them as mental disorders and compulsive behaviors without considering the possibility of them being satanically- inspired behavior that is passed from generation to generation. This makes conquering these behaviors a spiritual matter more so than medical or psychological. It is not to say that medicine or psychiatric treatment can't help, but it cannot cure.

Finally, real sexual intimacy has to be healthy, vivacious, and exempted from compulsive behavior which drives the romance far from the relationship. It must be rooted and driven by authentic love. An example of this sexual intimacy can be found in the

Song of Solomon or more correctly – the Song of Songs. Where the Shulamite woman who was Solomon's wife cries out, "I am my beloved's, And his desire is toward me." (Song of Solomon 7: 10) Even after the marriage is consummated, she makes it unambiguous that her husband still longs to be with her; he is not longing for the same gender, animals, or any other outlandish fetish. He is over-whelmed by passion for his wife and screaming for her to "Arouse me baby!" At the same time, she is screaming to him, "Romance me darling!" Both want the same thing, but his comes through the arousal technique with her touching his bare body, and hers comes through the romancing technique when he's caressing her, and speaking words descriptive of love. These factors work correctly when they stem from genuine love as the Song of Solomon 8: 7 has so eloquently spoken, "Many waters cannot quench love, nor can the floods drown it. If a man would give for love All the wealth of his house, It would be utterly despised." Yet, if every couple will strive to please their spouse every time they become sexually involved, then each one will always reach their highest climax and long to return to their sacred bedroom.

Bibliography

Adams, Jay E. Marriage, Divorce, and Remarriage. Grand Rapids, MI: Baker Book House, 1980.

Boone, Wellington. Your Wife is not Your Mama. New York, NY: Doubleday, 1999.

Custance, Arthur C. The Seed of the Woman. Lindsay, ON: Door way Publications, 1980.

Deen, Edith. All of the Women of the Bible. Edison, NJ: Castle Books, 1955.

Gray, John. Men are From Mars, Women are From Venus. New York, NY: Harper Collins Publishers, 1992.

Griffin, G. Edwards. The Creature from Jekyll Island: A Second Look at the Federal Reserve. Westlake Village, CA: American Media, 1994.

Groom, Nancy. Married Without Masks. Colorado Springs, CO: Navpress, 1989.

Handford, Elizabeth Rice. Me? Obey Him? Murfreesboro, TN: Sword of the Lord Publishers, 1994.

Lewis, Robert, and William Hendricks: Rocking the Roles: Building a Win-Win Marriage. Colorado Springs, CO: Navpress, 1991.

Love, Brenda. Encyclopedia of Unusual Sex Practices. New York, NY: Barricade Books Inc., 1992.

Shadkhan. Diictionary.com. © *Encyclopedia Britannica, Inc..*
Encyclopedia Britannica, Inc.. http://dictionary.reference.
com/browse/shadkhan (accessed: May 20, 2013).

Shema. Answers.com. The New Encyclopedia of Judaism, The
Jerusalem Publishing House, Ltd., 1989, 2002. http://www.
answers.com/topic/shema, accessed May 20, 2013.

Strong, James. The New Strong's Expanded Dictionary of Bible
Words. Nashville, TN: Thomas Nelson Publishers, 2001.

Traupman, John C. The Bantam New College Latin and English
Dictionary. 3rd ed. New York, NY: Bantam Dell, 2007.

Walker, Clarence. Breaking Strong Holds in the African-
American Family. Grand Rapids, MI: Zondervan Publishing
House, 1996.

Webster's New Collegiate Dictionary, ed. Henry B. Woolf.
Springfield, MA: G. & C. Merriam Co., 1979.

Wright, H. Norman. Communication: Key to Your Marriage.
Ventura, CA: Regal Books, 1980.